© **Uzochukwu Mike 2018**

Published by:

Self Publishing

United States

Dedication

To all Nigerian youths who work to reduce challenges among themselves, standing up for what is right, and bringing in good ideas that will help through positive development of the citizens of the country.

Acknowledgements

To Almighty God

My first acknowledgement goes to the Great Immortality of all immortals. He cannot be seen but can be felt. On my own I cannot do anything. God is the one that inspires and he inspired me before I could write on this book title.

To Muhammed Abdullahi Tosin

There are hidden talents in some persons yet to be discovered by people that possess such talents. Sometimes someone somewhere needs to touch these potentials before they can shine bright for people to see and benefit from them. Mr Muhammed Abdullahi Tosin touched the writing potential in me and it has shine out to the entire world. My written articles and books which have been read for over 1.7 million times by people from different parts of the world are made possible by you.

I did not know I could write until you organized essay contest in 2013 for students in different tertiary institutions in Nigeria. I participated in the contest and came out second nationwide after judgement. You made me discover the potential that has not been tapped into since birth. And from that day, I became an author that has attracted people both locally and internationally. I acknowledge your good heart dear Tosin.

To Amazon

My sincere gratitude goes to Jeff Bezos, the CEO of Amazon and the world richest man in 2018, for creating a platform where independent authors from different parts of the world publish their works to global market. I also acknowledge the entire Amazon team.

Contents

Chapter 1..1

Young Fraudsters in Nigeria (Yahoo or G Boys)

Chapter 2..7

Confirmed Incidences of G Boys

Chapter 3...15

Terms and Tricks used by Yahoo Boys

Chapter 4...58

How to avoid being a G Guy (Young

Fraudster)

Chapter 1

Young Fraudsters in Nigeria (Yahoo or G Boys)

The trend in Nigeria for about six years now is the fraudulent activities of G boys also known as yahoo boys. The high quest of Nigeria youths to make money has led them into criminal activities of so many kinds. Both the young and those who are already gaining sense of maturity want to make money either by crook or by hook. It is all about making money by some Nigerian youths irrespective of the source of the money.

Initially, the term Yahoo boy was connected with fraudsters who make money through dishonest means on the internet. There are several proven crooked schemes such people use while striving for immense wealth (Madaily Gist 2018). Yahoo boys in Nigeria are overshadowed with get rich quick syndrome. That is why you can see a young boy of 20 years already wearing very expensive wrist watches, necklaces, and even driving expensive cars.

Nigeria records about N127 billion loss annually to cyber-crime. In 2014 alone, the anti-graft agency – Economic and Financial Crimes Commission, EFCC reported that customers in Nigeria lost about N6 billion to cyber criminals. Banks in Nigeria have lost approximately N159 billion to electronic frauds and cyber-crimes between 2000 and 2013.

According to a report by Ultrascan AGI, a subsidiary of Ultrascan Research Services – an international research organization, a whopping sum of $12.7 billion was lost to Nigerian scams (focusing on Advance Fee Fraud statistics) in 2013. In 2012, losses totaled $10.9 billion from $9.6 billion in 2011. Another report says that $50 million is lost annually to romance scams which our brothers participate actively in (OsayimwenOsahon George 2018). Some after falling victim of internet scam by fraudsters ended up committing suicide. Examples of such persons are Marjorie Earl Jones of United States of America and Ian Doney of United Kingdom.

Yahoo Boys are ready to disrespect any elder that try to advise them to stop the fraud they are into. To these young boys, taking advice from any elderly or wise men in their society is making them to be old fashioned. To them, they are current fashioned working with current civilization in the society.

These fraudsters who operate on the internet are making the internet unsafe for the users. They are on social media sites of various kinds. Some of them who are on dating sites claim to be who they are not. Some Nigerian G boys register on dating sites and give themselves fine European and American names. They sometimes make claim like they are Italians living in United Kingdom. They meet foreign women on dating sites and play on their intelligence and at the end dupe them large amount of money. They have many tricks they use.

Some parents who love money irrespective of the source are happy to see their children make money through fraudulent ways. Some fathers are beginning to send their children to experienced scammers in the society to learn how to do scams. All they want is for their children to make money whether the money is clean or not. Some will tell you that there is nothing like clean money. To them, "all die na die". It means that all deaths are death. They are careless about the source of the money.

The pitiable thing is that the G boys in town are going diabolic. It is no longer tricks as usual. Some of them are into rituals. They are ready to make sacrifices of human just to make money. They now kill their fellow humans all in the name that they want to gain power to make money.

That is intellectual poverty that many of them are suffering from. Human life is very expensive but most yahoo boys do not want to hear that. Their hands are soaked in blood. Blood and rituals waste everywhere. Some of them have gone extra mile. They have gone very far to acquire devilish power so that any of their victims they tell to send any amount of money will do that without any questions. They are the young evil men in Nigeria recently. But one thing is sure: there is no peace for the wicked. Souls that they have condemned will come for them.

In this section of this book, we `will be using Yahoo boys, G boys,

Yahoo guys, G guys, fraudsters and internet scammers interchangeably. Whenever we use any of these terms just know that we are talking about the same set of persons. They are same persons with so many names because they claim to be smart.

Chapter 2

Confirmed Incidences of G Boys

There are instances of the activities of G boys in Nigeria. Their activities which are bad have been published by news reporting companies. A young man identified as Leeroy Egebe was arrested and arraigned in court by the Economic and Financial Crimes Commission (EFCC) in Warri, Delta state for duping a Swiss woman of N81m. He was arraigned on 8-count charge bordering on conspiracy and obtaining money from a Swiss woman by false pretence (Adunni Amodeni 2018).

Because of the high quest for money, these men do not mind using people they pretend they love for money. This is evident in the news report by a newspaper company in Nigeria whereby a young male student who is an internet fraudster used his girlfriend for ritual. Some of them are into this devilish act so that they can make more money from their victims. Also, some do this to fortify themselves and become richer.

One young G boy used the girlfriend for ritual in early 2018. This was reported by The Guardian News, thus "daughter of the immediate past deputy governor of Ondo State, Alhaji Olugbenga Oluboyo, who was reported missing, Miss Adenike Khadijat, has been found dead in Akure, the state capital. The late Khadijat was found dead under the bed of her Abuja-based boyfriend, Adeyemi Alao, in Oke-Aro area of the city on Thursday, after she was murdered allegedly for money rituals (Oluwaseun Akingboye and

Ruth Omasheye 2018)". The lady used by the wicked boyfriend was a 400 level student of Adekunle Ajasin University, Akungba Akoko. Ladies are advised to be careful of the kind of men they have as their boyfriends. All that glitters is not gold.

The most annoying thing is that upon all these evils happening in the society, ladies still follow the young men that they know have no legal jobs to their homes. Why should a lady follow a young man that has no personal legal jobs to their homes? Because of the love for money, many have been killed and some have their virginal fluids cleaned for rituals unknown to them. Ladies should be careful and stop being foolish because of material things they will enjoy for few days and it is over. It is annoying to see ladies with big heads and no wisdom or ability to think well and make right decisions before taking any step.

In the year 2017, Nairaland community reported news on how two Nigerian Yahoo boys scammed Nigerian American businessman.

The business man was a Nigerian but does his business in United States of America. The money the two fraudsters duped him in the name that they are land owners was approximately N787million (seven hundred and eighty seven million Nigeria naira).

"A US-based Nigerian businessman was dazed in Lagos, when land agents led him to the lagoon after the part-payment for 150 plots offered for N787.5 million. Kennedy Chukwuemeka Nwabuoku told detectives led by DCP Abutu Yaro, at the Force Criminal Investigations and Intelligence Department (FCIID), Alagbon, how he had paid N577, 590, 792 in instalments among other charges, plus another N18million for bush clearing in February, and how the agents were sending him pictures and videos of caterpillars in action at the purported site at Ifedele Agunbiade village, Sangotedo, in Eti-Osa area of Lagos.

Nwabuoku told the police that he bought the unseen land with a foreign partner and had paid in fiduciary trust, sending monies on different occasions through his company, Ken Bouk Global Investment Ltd. Identified as Emeka Okoronkwo and Michael Owolabi Alonge, the agents, according to Nwabuoku, had offered the land for sale at N5, 250, 000 per plot with Certificate of Occupancy (Ahamefuna 2017)". These yahoo boys are so tricky to the extent that they can open business accounts with unique names. They are smart but some of them have been caught irrespective of their smartness.

Their smartness makes their works appear to be real but they are faked. Most people fall prey to them because of the level of their packaging. Many people are victims because of their mindsets that it is a company and not individual accounts that they paid to. Some people who they duped paid into the company accounts they created and today the victims cannot see what they paid for. That is the game and that is why they are called G boys.

Nothing can be compared with human life. What is bad is bad. A criminal act is a criminal act and nothing can change that. Also, a wicked act is a wicked and no amount of "baptism" can change it from being what it is. Whether they baptize them G boys, Yahoo boys or Yahoo plus, they are all internet scammers.

The most painful wicked activity of G boys in the year 2018 in Nigeria was the one that happened in Delta State University, Abraka. The wickedness of these young men shook the entire city of Abraka and the country at large. Till tomorrow, the community will not forget that pain.

That was the kidnap and killing of a bright female student of the department of Mass Communication of the university. The student though in 300 level maintained First Class grade. That was a distinction. Irrespective of the great brain possessed by this student who name was Elozino Ogege, the yahoo boys kidnapped and killed her for ritual. Elizino was loved by all. She was dedicated to her studies, respectful, accommodating and always ready to teach her fellow students.

From the report from Vanguard News on November 19, 2018, the company wrote in these sentences:

"The discovery of the late student happened on the same day residents of Umono Street in Abraka, Ethiope East Local Government Area of Delta State discovered the lifeless body of a two-year-old male child abandoned near an electricity transformer. The student, Elozino Ogege, had been declared missing after she was said to have gone out to meet an agent who was assisting her secure an apartment for her with plans of relocating to another part of the university town.

Sources in the area who identified the victim, told Vanguard that she was a 300 level student of the Department of Mass Communication. One of the sources, who simply gave his name as Michael, said: "Her decomposing corpse was found on Friday with her tongue and breast severed from her body (Perez Brisibe

2018)". The Yahoo boys who are coded ritualists used the bright lady by cutting away her breast and tongue.

They drive flashy cars round the town and little do their fellow students know that some of them have soiled their hands in human blood. They are evil blood suckers that fulfil their evil plans in the dark. They are evil boys.

Chapter 3

Terms and Tricks used by Yahoo Boys

Yahoo boys in Nigeria talk in codes. There are some terms they use when they discuss among one another and sometimes on the streets. These slangs sometimes sound sweet in ears but some of them are dangerous. They use them in their everyday dirty business and sometimes when they enter banks to pick the money sent to them by the person they duped.

In the same way, there are some tricks used by internet scammers in Nigeria which people who live and outside the country do not know. Because many people do not have knowledge of these their tricks, they became victims of their tricks. This chapter is written to serve as eye opener to a lot of people all over the globe. Any who goes through this updated book chapter will hardly fall prey to the tricks used by internet fraudsters from Nigeria.

Terms Used by Yahoo Boys (Internet Fraudsters)

Clients

Clients to yahoo boys are people who are victims of their scam. Also, clients can imply some people they are working on to succumb to their scam tricks. You hear them make statements like "my client from United States of America did not pay well this time around". Again, they make statement like "how I wish this my client will pay up to six thousand dollars ($6,000)". Those that have buoyant clients live well because they (the clients) always send money to them in Nigeria from United States or other developed countries.

Voltage

This means how rich a particular person is. A person whose voltage is high is someone who has much money. When a yahoo boy tells you that that his client has a full voltage, what it implies is that the client has much money. The money made by the foreign client can be because he or she does a good job.

Level

It is a slang used by yahoo boys which can mean anything. Outside G guys, it is used commonly by people in different cities of the country. Maybe a yahoo guy told his friend who is into same scam that he is expecting money from a client, later when they meet, the friend may ask how was the level? Meaning how did the business go?

Bomb

Bomb as a term used by internet scammers in Nigeria can mean hack or to hack. When a Yahoo boy says that he is bombing, what it means is that he is hacking. When he says he is searching for a Facebook account to bomb what it means is that he is searching for a Facebook account to hack. When they bomb any of users Facebook accounts, they take over the accounts to carryout their scam.

Mugu

Mugu is a Nigerian word for those who fall victim to Yahoo boys' trick. It implies a fool as well. Also, it is used generally in the country as those who are not wise. Also, the term "mugu" can mean to fall sheepishly to something. Example of the sentence that involves the use of this term is "do you know that the mugu still paid extra five hundred dollars thinking that I am real" Another is "do you know that guy falls mugu to that lady? "

Maga

The term maga implies the person that falls to the scam of the Yahoo boys. It is similar to mugu. It is used interchangeably with mugu. As someone who stays in the environment filled with these scammers, you hear them make sentence like "has the maga pay?" What it means whether the person they planned to scam has paid any money. Maga is the derogatory term used to refer to a foreigner that fall victim to internet fraud schemes of Nigerian fraudsters. These scammers sometimes speak in codes so that a novice will not understand their plans.

Tricks used by Young Nigerian Internet Fraudsters

They have many ways through which they trap their victims. If they apply plan A and it does not work, they apply plan B and C. But no matter the approach these Yahoo boys use, you cannot fall prey to them if you are careful and up to date. It is important to get information on what is happening in your society every point in time. Also, foreigners have to be wise on their own to prevent being used as Automated Teller Machine (ATM) by these young scammers.

Operation on Social Media sites

They sign up on social media sites with false identity. They sign up on Twitter for example bearing the names of celebrities. They usually do this using the names of foreign artists and actors that are well known.

At first, they try to follow some persons from Europe and United

States of America. They may follow about ten thousand white people. After some time, the persons they followed initially on twitter follow them back. Not all will follow but at least reasonable number of persons. Their target is usually people abroad and also those who are working.

When the internet fraudsters who pretends to be someone also observed that some persons they followed before have followed them back, they, the fraudsters, hiding under the image of celebrities go and unfollow others. Doing this make them have more followers. In this case, they have more followers than the people they follow.

At that point, they began to make their intelligent plans for those they will defraud. They began to build webs in which they will use to trap their victims. A scammer who set up a twitter of a Canadian singer Justin Drew Bieber for example follows the activities of the singer properly. If he is to go for a show, the scammer makes an earlier update on that. When he performs in the show, the scammer also showcases that on twitter handle as well. With time, people begin to believe that he is the real Justin Drew Bieber.

Everything looks real but it is all scam. The fraudster just acquired the identity of the real artist. He impersonates the real artists and makes the whole thing looks real. With time, he begins to penetrate the followers.

He may start by twitting that he has a project he is planning to start. He tells the followers that the project is a multi million dollars business. He goes ahead and persuades the followers to invest in the project that after a month of completion of the project, every investor will be paid back with increase of about 200% of their invested capital. Yahoo boys can paint pictures and make every of their plans look attractive and colourful.

When they capture the attention of some of the followers, the business becomes half done. The scammer presents his account details to those that are ready to invest into the project that he claimed. As time goes on, he updates the victims of the progress in the proposed project. The victims believe that everything is real but little do they know that they have been duped by a scammer who lives in one city in Nigeria. He may screen grab beautiful pictures of an ongoing project in a place and upload it to the victims to show them the progress. Also, they sometimes source for pictures from different websites.

When the time he initially told his victims that the project will be completed has come, he may cook another story telling them that everything did not work as planned. He persuades them to invest more and that the return they will get at the end will be much higher. Some of them still pay into the account given to them by the G boy that pretends to be the artist. The young man goes to the bank and withdraws the money and continues to live large while the fooled are hoping that they will get huge return at the right.

At the end when the claimed artist is expected to pay his investors, he backs off. He blocks those whom he scammed on the twitter social media site. Sometimes, they send messages to the victims saying "you have just been duped by a black man". But some of the scammers after duping their clients blocks them on twitter and even delete their own accounts.

The victims regret for their entire life after being scammed of huge amount of money. They cry in silence and curse the person that duped them. They made big mistake they never believed they would. G boys live expensive lives while the victims are in agony.

Sometimes, they hack into the twitter accounts of prominent people and extort money from the friends. So many twitter users have lost a lot of money through twitter by falling prey to the users. It is sad to hear that the social media site is not safe any longer. It hurts many people in our society today.

Yahoo Boys scam through Facebook

Facebook is another social media site that G boys use to defraud users. One of the ways through which they do this is by creating Facebook accounts with fake details. They have so many ways they use to dupe people on Facebook.

They can create the account with fake information. A yahoo boy may use the name of a lady and pretends to be the person on the profile picture. He may go and source the pictures of a porn star. He shows the nudity of the lady he is impersonating on his walls pretending to be woman that can always give her body to any man for sex.

He then send friends request to many Facebook users. Some of the users that receive the request accept. Men are moved by what they see with their eyes and because of this many quickly accept the request once they see the exposed body. Some who are aware of their tricks after checking on the profile picture of the scammer declines the request. But those that accept with the mindset that the request was sent to them by a lady that is ready to have sweet sex with them in the long run put themselves in great danger.

The 'sexy lady' in disguise then begins to chat with the Facebook friends. At first she introduces herself as a particular person (note that sometimes it is a man but pretends to be woman, so understand when we use 'she'). She then begins to tell the prospective victim how sexy she is and how she can be so naughty in bed. At the end, she may tell the man that she will like to visit so that they can have fun at night. Some of them pretend to be students that have time for visit during the weekend.

If she is able to capture the attention of thee man by making the man lusty, she is close to achieving her aim which is defrauding the man of money. Some of these G boys capture the attention of their victims by sending them pornographic pictures of the woman they pretend to be. Also, some of them send short videos of where they are fingering themselves and appears to be so naughty.

The next step after capturing the attention of the victim by making the man to be emotionally high is to demand for the transport fare she will use to come down. The young man pretending to be a hot lady may tell the man that 'she' is coming from a far place. The essence is because 'she' wants to make good amount of money from the man.

The man demands for 'her' account number and it was sent. 'She' may send an account number bearing another lady's name and tell the man to pay in that 'her' own account is dormant. They can cook stories that appear to be real. That is what makes them scammers.

After the transport money has been sent, the next demand can be money to buy clothes to wear for the visit. 'She' may tell the man that all her clothes are old. When succeeded in convincing the man for the money for clothes and then sent again, she promises the man that she will be coming next weekend.

The heart of the man gladdens and he keeps preparing for the unknown lady that will arrive in the next weekend for them to have great sex. But little did he know that the person he had been chatting with is a man pretending to be a woman. When the faithful day for the appointment comes, the lady will not show up. The man chats with the lady asking for explanation and she gives an excuse.

At this point 'she' may tell the man that she had accident. All is the tricks they work with. After excuses upon excuses, the victim becomes tired. After much pressure from the man, the scammer may block the man and there will be no conversation between them again. The money the man sent is gone. That is Nigerian G boys for you. They can play on people's emotions. Some of them are good at that.

Another way through which these bad guys scam people on Facebook is by hacking into the users account. They have been doing this and have been succeeding for years now. It is advised that everyone that does not want to have his or her Facebook account hacked should use strong password. Also, it is not advisable to login into your Facebook accounts using public computer, for example logging in through computers used in Cyber Café.

Internet scammers can lay their hands on the same computer you just finished making use of and changed your password unknown to you if you did not log out before you left. And sometimes your browsing time expires why browsing at Cyber Café and you could not log out before you leave. You consider the money you will spend in buying another time and you decide to leave.

Some people wake up in the morning and tried logging in to their Facebook accounts but could not do that. What is the meaning of this? What really happened? I cannot login again but I know my password. Sorry, someone somewhere has acquired your Facebook account. It is gone. Someone else has taken control and that is a G guy that may come from Nigeria. It is their job. They hunt for accounts to hack every blessed day.

Do not use your phone number as your password on Facebook. That is how they acquired so many accounts of the users of the social media. Some people use their phone numbers as their passwords for easy remembrance but it is not healthy. Your Facebook account can easily get hacked when you adopt such approach. Your password should be mixture of alphabet, numbers, and special characters. This will make it difficult for yahoo guys to hack your Facebook account.

Also, the use of your date of birth as password is risky as well. It makes your account vulnerable for internet scammers to penetrate. It should be elements that their minds will be difficult to get.

When the internet fraudsters take control of the account of an active user, they can go far in getting what they need. They first go through the messages of the person they hacked the account. This makes them to discover the persons' the user chats always. Their next step becomes money demands. They may send messages to one of the major persons demanding for money and to pay back within certain intervals.

When the person did not confirm by calling the person that demands and sends the requested amount, the scammer goes and withdraw the money. He may frame a story that he was in a particular place and should send the money to another person's account. But the victim may not know that the account number given to him was the impersonator account number. He still meets others by sending messages requesting for monetary assistance. Other people send the money with the mindset that their friend is in need.

Before many discovered that they were scammed that the account of their friend was impersonated by a fraudster, it had already become late. The scammer had already made good amount of money from them before his victims found out. Yahoo boys are threat to Facebook social media today.

Some of these fraudsters adopt the approach of creating groups on Facebook and claim that the groups are non-governmental organizations. They claim that the groups are located in a particular region in a country. Some may say that a non-governmental organization located in Oakland in United States of America with a particular name is taking care of some people who are suffering from serious sickness. They go further by saying that the members of the group need to donate money even as small as 20 dollars to save the dying.

The G boys/guys paint the picture of the whole thing as if it is real but it is not. They regularly upload the pictures of those they claim are dying and need financial assistance. Those who are ignorant of the activities of these scammers fall prey to their packaged story.

Take for example that among two thousand members of the group, that 800 persons donates 20 dollars each, that is a good amount of money. If you multiply 800 by 20 dollars, it will give a total amount of 16,000 dollars. That is total of sixteen thousand US dollars. If the G guy is from Nigeria, the young man made approximately 5.7 million naira from the scam. That's a dubious act that makes them spend money lavishly. Beware of Yahoo boys from Nigeria. Confirm any information you see on Facebook as well as other social media sites.

The rate of moral decay in Federal Republic of Nigeria is very high. So many Nigerians takes the things of God for levity. Some of these young fraudsters have claimed to be pastors or priests of churches in Nigeria just to dupe people good amount of money. That is devilish.

A powerful and famous Catholic priest Rev. Fr Ejike Mbaka has been impersonated by the G guys on social media, particularly

Facebook and these wicked souls have dupe Nigerians home and abroad using the name of the man of God. When this crime got to the ear of Fr. Mbaka, he voiced that he was not the one. He said that he was not on Facebook and those who used his name for such atrocity will suffer unless they repent. As of the time of publication of this work, Rev. Fr. Ejike Mbaka of Adoration Ministry Enugu has no Facebook account of any kind.

In the year 2018, it was gathered that Reverend Father Ejike Mbaka caught one of the fraudsters who have been using his name to scam people. The report shows that the young man was an ex-seminarian. It was painful to hear that.

"The Spiritual Director, Adoration Ministry, Enugu Nigeria, Rev. Fr. EjikeMbaka has exposed a man who has allegedly been using his name to scam people. It was gathered that the man, an ex-seminarian, hails from Imo State. The ex-seminarian has been scamming people in Awka with Father Mbaka's name until he was caught. In a video, Mbaka, however, brought the man to his Adoration Ministry Enugu ground and exposed him completely in front of the congregation (Don Silas 2018)".

This is for someone who impersonated him physically. There are many who has impersonated him online including Facebook and have not been caught till date. They are intelligent Yahoo guys.

Nigerian Youth Scammers on Dating Sites

It is their jobs. They are good at it. They have duped many people and are still going to dupe more for thousands of dollars. They go into dating sites searching for working white ladies they will scam to make money. The category of white women that fall victim are those who are adults but still need men to stay with. Some of them are those who were divorced. Some of them are advanced women but want to satisfy their sexual desires and others need men to answer their names. They want to get married.

Young Fraudsters in Nigeria (Yahoo or G Boys)

These young men can be in Nigeria and still have foreign phone numbers. They paid for these phone numbers to the telecommunication companies in United States and other foreign countries and have the ability to use them here in Nigeria. When you call them on the foreign numbers they answer and communicate well with you.

So, do not be surprised if they give foreign number and you call and communicated with them. Also, some of them have voice changing applications installed in their phones. If they pretend to be women and the men who are victims call them, they speak like women to the men with the help of the voice changing application installed in their phones.

Nigerian G boys enter dating sites claiming who they are not just because they want to make money in a dubious way. Some claim to be Italians working in United Kingdom while others claim something else. They paint good pictures of who they claim to be.

What is important to them is that they make their money at the end.

After being friends with the women they want to scam, they began to discuss. Their first approach is to know what the women do. This will make them to find out if the women can give them the amount of money they need in the long run. The reason is because they must make attempt to scam the prospect. That is their main reason for being on the site.

As days goes on, they began to go deeper into erotic chat. They can go into sex chat with the women they pretend to love. This makes their prospect feel horny and their attention captured.

The criminals who are the G boys in this context go deeper and deeper. They do not mind dropping their nude photos to the women every early morning. This makes the women feel that their 'men' love them so much. They have been captured emotionally if the clients begins to feel this way.

With time, the G guy may tell the 'lover' that he was not feeling well and that he needed about one thousand dollars for treatment. The woman began to source for money because she needed to save the lover who is a coded Yahoo guy. In this state, the guy speaks as if he is really sick. He knows his job.

She gets the money and sends to him. The woman who did that had in mind that her lover would come and marry her when everything is in place. The G boy continues to extort money from the victim he got online. The scam continues until the woman realizes herself and stops sending money to him.

To show you how powerful these Yahoo boys are; some of them can control the women to leave their home countries to Nigeria just for them to come and see these fake lovers. There are such incidences. When they come, they lodge in hotels making love with their fake lovers until they go back to their home countries. What make the women to come down to see their "lovers" is usually because they have waited for a long time without seeing their "lovers" in real life and touching them. They want to feel them through sexual contact and be happy.

How G boys scam people as investors and project executors

They have many ways they adopt to dupe people. Some of them claim to be investors and encourage others to invest with them claiming they will pay back with mouth watering interests. It is completely faked. They are not real. They just want to go away with your hard earned money.

Investing can be a minefield for beginners and experienced traders alike. Not only do beginners have to learn new financial instruments and trading lingo, but they also have to be on guard against the slew of scammers and fraudsters seeking to prey on novice traders. Similarly experienced traders can become victims because as their confidence becomes complacency (Lawrence Pines 2018).

Nigerian internet fraudsters set up brokers sites claiming to be real and searching for investors. They sometimes go into online communities in search for some foreigners who are well to do and need ways to maximize their profits. When they meet these clients, they confuse them by telling them that they have ongoing projects that need investors. They can tell their 'preys' that if they are able to invest in a particular country, they have high return in terms of interest within the next 20 days.

For example, a Nigerian G guy can tell his client that if he invests in United States, he will get the invested money with interest of 20% within 20 days. But if the investor invests in Nigeria, he will get the capital with interest of about 120% within 20 days. That is the trick.

Because everyone likes interest, he decides to invest in Nigeria. But do you know the trick behind the game? The reason why the scammer gives higher interest for Nigeria is because he can easily pick the money in the country. There will no stress. But if the investor chooses to invest in a country like United States, he may not make much gain. The thing is that when the victim sends the money to United States, the fraudster has to look for someone that will receive the money over there in United States of America for him. And the person who receives the money is paid some percentages as he sends the money down to the Yahoo boy in Nigeria after picking the money through Western Union, MoneyGram or through any other channel.

That is how the scam goes on. When it is time for the scammer to pay the defrauded, he cooks a sweet story for the victim. Some of them delete their account from the site after scamming two or three persons. The money becomes lost and not traced.

Worldwide $16 billion was lost to various types of fraud, scams and identity theft in 2016. This represents a 16% increase over 2015 and is the highest level of fraud recorded since Javelin

Strategy & Research (the firm behind the report) began tracking this statistic in 2004. Fraud affects every region of the globe and manifests itself in many different forms (ibid).

These Yahoo boys are bad boys. Another way through which they scam people online is through Binary. They search for investors as well here. They work tirelessly day and night sourcing for ways to make money. These young Nigerian men think far to get their jobs done in intelligent ways. Some of them are technologically sound.

A binary option is a financial exotic option in which the payoff is either some fixed monetary amount or nothing at all. Binary has been corrupted by Nigerian youths who are scammers. Many binary option outlets have been exposed as fraudulent (Federal Bureau of Investigation). The U.S. FBI is investigating binary option scams throughout the world, and the Israeli police have tied the industry to criminal syndicates.

Nigerian youths are into binary but their aim for going into that is to scam people. They do go into that not to do clean business but to dupe investors and run away. They have sugar coated tongues but are coded criminals. Their hands are not clean at all.

When they meet investors, they persuade them to invest in a particular project and get mouth watering interest within a certain period of time. They send the details of payment to the investor and he sends the money down to Nigeria. The young fraudster bounces into Nigerian bank and pick up the money through any abroad money receiving channels.

When the agreed time for the investor to receive the capital and the interest for the investment has reached, the investor receives an alert that a particular amount of money has been credited to his account/wallet. This alert is engineered by the Nigerian scammer. The client logs in and sees the money. But for him to collect the money and spend he could not. It looks surprising to him (the victim).

He walks into the bank to complain of the issue and the bank tells him that the fault is not from them but from the broker (the sender of the money). The duped writes back to the 'scammer' pretending to be a broker. The "broker" tell him that he needs to pay for signal for the money to be accessible by him. These bad guys sometimes put fear in their victims by telling them that if they don't pay, the money they have invested will be lost.

They are wicked souls that have no human sympathy. Because the investor do not want to loose the huge amount of money he has invested, he goes and pay for the so called "signal". There is nothing like "signal" payment but the scammer did that to steal more money from the victim. After payment, the scammer confirms the transaction. Now he may send few amounts of dollars that his 'prey' can have access to. He gets bank alert on that and feels that everything will take shape with time. He makes attempt to withdraw the money and it works. But he has not yet been able to have access to the main good amount of money. The money is not yet accessible.

The victim writes back that he received the one sent but not yet able to access the first money sent to him which includes the main capital and the interest. The G guy apologizes and tells him that the technicians are still working on the issue that he would have access to all his money soon. Coded criminal in quote is the G boy.

After few days, the scammer writes back to the investor telling him that he has to pay for Access as soon as possible. He may add fire to the duped foreigner that everything will be lost if he does not act fast. It's a pity. Men playing on the intelligence of others are bad men.

The victim does everything possible to make sure that he meets up. He gathers the money and makes the transfer expecting everything will work out finally. Once the victim sends the money, the fraudster goes to the bank and withdraws the money.

The next is that he goes to the site and deprives the victim access to the site. The victim of the binary scam would not have access to the site again not to talk of communicating with the scammer again. That is the wickedness among Nigerian young scammers. It is evil. Someone is somewhere enjoying another man's money and the duped cries bitterly. Man's inhumanity to man.

You have to be careful on how you believe things you see online in order to be safe. Do not register on every website you see. Some of them are there to get your personal details. Verify to know the authenticity of the site. Some that you meet online and they tell you they are looking for investors or are searching for investors are fake people. They are not real. They are searching for who they will defraud.

Bitcoin which is the trending is becoming faked. Yahoo boys are defrauding many people through this channel. They know how to manipulate some people. They are good manipulators. They tell you they have Bitcoin to sell that you should credit them. Once you credit them in dollars, they block you and you lose your money. You cannot get the Bitcoin equivalent of the dollars you paid to them.

ATM card hack (Local Operation) by G boys

They rush into the bank crying. They cried to the customer care section of the bank complaining of what happened to them. Some of them are students while others are old women who cannot read or write. They were pitied by the staff of the bank. But at the end, nothing could be done for the recovery of the money. The customers have lost their hard earned money to Nigeria young scammers. Some are being told of the process to pass through which among them is reporting to police station to know if they could get their money back but many are afraid of going to the police to report. The security sector of Nigeria is messed up, so some victims of local scam see going to police stations to report as means of losing more money.

So many people are in fear because of the actions of these young criminals. When the customers who were duped by them are crying, they, the scammers, are somewhere already partying with the money they stole from poor women and men in the country.

Tell me how nemesis will not catch up with the criminals. After stealing from poor people in the country intentionally, you come out calling yourself a big guy. A criminal is a criminal and that is what they are.

The worst is that some of these people they dupe are helpless students whom their parents struggled hard to gather the money and sent across to them for school fees. And a coded young man who calls himself a yahoo boy use tricks to steal. There are so many things God will judge; criminals being happy at the bitterness of other people.

Many Nigerians are even afraid to have their money in the bank as a result of the rate of scam going on in the country. Many of our youths do not want to work again. What they want is hot money. And the funny thing is that they do not know some of this hot money kills.

One of the ways they scam people locally in the country is by sending messages to account holders in the banks telling them that their accounts have been blocked. Some of them read that the ATM card has been blocked. Some send text messages using the bank's title telling their prospects that their BVN is blocked. They further persuade the receiver of the message to call a particular number. It is a common scam carried out by the young scammers in Nigeria.

They have a unique way of constructing the scam messages. An example of the message they use to scam people reads thus: "Dear Customer, due to the BVN validation in compliance with CBN directives, your ATM card has been deactivated. Call our helpline on 08034138959 now".

Once the receiver of the message calls and follows the instructions given to him by the coded criminal, the money in his account gets debited within few minutes. When the receiver calls the phone number he is instructed to call, the person pretending to be a customer care agent calls his name. This makes the prospective victim to believe that the person he called was a customer care agent of the bank.

The prospective victim of local scam will be like "since this young man called my name, he will be from the bank for sure. But little did he know that someone that knows him maybe the person that supplied his full name to the scammer. Also, there are applications that can detect peoples' names which many people are not aware of. That is the game. That is the scam. The fraudster pretending to be an agent of the bank asks the receiver of the message few questions including the last time he used his ATM card.

When the man supply the information the scammer needs, he smiles that he is making headway in the criminal trick. He is further asked to call out his card number and the ATM card pin. If he does that, the work of the scammers are almost done. The scammer tells the prospective victim of the scam that a five digits pin will be sent to him to fasten the activation process and once that is done that he should send him the pin.

Immediately that pin is sent to him and he sends it or calls it to the hearing of the scammer, he turns from prospective victim to full victim. At this point, the money of the victim becomes debited from his account. What the scammers did was that they installed mobile application on the phones they "use for their businesses" and then transfer the customer's money to another account of their choice. Many Nigerians are victims of this kind of fraud. Some Mobile Applications can transfer maximum of one million naira in a day in Nigerian banks.

In Nigeria, many businesses have fold because many Nigerians are victim of this kind of fraud. Some loss the money they use for their businesses to these wicked souls that call themselves Yahoo boys. They are big time criminals. They take advantage of people that are not informed.

Since this kind of scam became rampant in the country, banks have been sending notifications to customers not to disclose their card numbers and pins to people. Irrespective of the notifications, many are still falling victims. Some who cannot read and have account numbers are still victims to the challenge. It is a big challenge in the country. Some who can read are always in a hurry to read through short messages sent to them by their individual banks. Even when some are in banks and the staffs want to educate them on important information, many do not pay attention because they are always in a hurry to go.

G boys hack into bank customers account

This kind of hack is highly technical. These bad boys have grown to the level of hacking into accounts of bank customers. It is difficult to know if these boys have insider in the banks that help them carryout this kind of bad action or they have applications that are so rugged to break into some customers account.

In this kind of fraud by G guys, they target rich men in the society. They do this because they know they will make good amount of money if they succeed in doing so. It is a risky stealing. It is risky in the sense that if they are caught they will end their lives in prisons.

When these criminals have access into customers account, their first move is to change certain information in the account. These include the original phone number and email address of the account holders. Sometimes, they deactivate them so that the owner of the account will not receive any alert or notifications on what goes on in their accounts.

Gradually, they begin to move the money in the victim accounts to their own accounts. Also, sometimes they move the money to their friend accounts or to accounts of people they have met before. They may call someone for his account number so that they can empty the accounts of their victims.

It is advised that customers should not give their account details to people they do not know too well. Even if you know the person as a scammer, never give your account details to him or her. It is risky to do that. The reason is that they may put you into trouble.

If you give your account number to scammers or people you do not know, they may make transfer of money obtained through dubious way to your account. When this happens, you may not know. Your bank account may be monitored until you go to the bank to withdraw money.

At that point when you want to make withdrawal without knowing that your account is monitored, security officials will come and arrest you. You pass through stress for what you do not know much about. Being a financial crime, you may be imprisoned. Until you are able to provide the G guy that hacked the customer's account and made the transfer to you, you will not be released. Suffering for another person's bad action is bad but the bank cannot help until you provide the scammer. It is usually painful.

Another approach that Yahoo boys used to hack into bank customers account was published by The Guardian Newspaper Company in the year 2017. The narration given by the newspaper company showed that some yahoo boys are computer experts. They are technically sound in their operation. The company through the write-up of Samson stated:

"They work in multiple ways, such as sending mails to victims, local or international, purportedly from banks, persuading them to enrol on an offer that would ultimately grant the fraudsters access to hack into the victim's accounts.

At this stage, the victim receives a link purportedly from the bank that automatically redirects to the Internet banking portal, where the fraudsters clone the webpage, despite the fact that banks are not supposed to have access to a customer's Internet banking password.

The fraudster is aware whenever the link is opened and every information entered is seen and watched backend. The scammer then opens the victim's bank authentic Internet banking platform and keys in the username and password entered to login, initiate an Internet banking transfer and waits for the OTP (one time password) to complete it.

At the point when the victim types in his or her OTP on the cloned website, the fraudster completes the first transfer immediately. If the victim doesn't get an alert of the debit, the scammer initiates another transfer and waits for the victim to enter another OTP and then completes the second transfer (The Guardian news 2017)".

Chapter 4

How to avoid being an Internet Fraudster

(Young Fraudster)

Some people who are into scam today were not there before. Something pushed them into it and they are tagged scammers today. Everyone wants to make quick money. Everyone frwants to live good when there is availability of money. If you want to avoid being a Yahoo boy, there are some qualities and virtues you have to possess. They include contentedness, self discipline, patience, self confidence, mindfulness of groups, and avoiding envy.

Contentedness

What is contentedness? The term contentedness means to be satisfied with things as they are. It is to be satisfied with the things you have right now as you hope for better tomorrow. The youths in Nigeria and those abroad need to have it.

They need to possess it to live at peace. When a youth is not contented with the properties and what he has, he begins to look for alternatives on how to make money either by crook or by hook. Because of this, he may find himself in the midst of scammers in his society. But when you are satisfied with where you are today, you have no reason for being a scammer because of money.

Youths should learn how to be happy in their current stage in life. They have to thank their Maker for making them who they are today. They have to show sign of gratitude. When you are happy with yourself, you do not need to be moved to do dirty things because of money.

Self discipline

If you are well disciplined in life, you will not be moved when you see some fraudulent actions people take to make money. Self discipline will make you see these young fraudsters in your country as people who do not know what they are doing. You perceive them as people who are senseless because what goes around comes around.

This is because when one dupes someone whom he feels is a novice to make money, in one way or the other, he will still spend the money. Again, there will be a point the scammer will get in life, he feels bitter of the bad things he did in the past. He will not have rest of mind. And when you are discipline, you stick on what is right and always do it well. Self discipline brings self respect. When you respect yourself, you do not do things that will make people disrespect you. A scammer is not respected.

Mindfulness of Groups

It is not all groups that worth being a member of. There are some groups you do not need to be a partaker of irrespective of how attractive the group may appear to be. There is a saying that bad company corrupts good manner. This saying is true because if rotten fruits are in contact with the good ones for a long time, at a point the bacteria that attacks the bad ones gets transferred to attack the good ones.

If you do not want to be initiated into the group of Yahoo boys in Nigeria, avoid their group. Also, you have to avoid being a member of groups that have Yahoo boys as part of them. When you associate with the group consisting of their members, when they discuss money and begin to call big amounts of money that they made through their scam, you can be tempted to join them. The amount of money you heard them calling may keep ringing in your brain until you start to ask them how they do it.

It takes strong discipline for you not to ask them. But if you are strongly moved to ask them how they make their money, they can teach you their tricks. When they teach you their dubious ways of making money and they sink into your brain joined with you practicing it, automatically you become a G guy. Everyone begins to see you as one of the young men that use dubious ways to make money from people.

Yahoo boys can be intimidating. If you start comparing their wealth with yours, you may quit the legal job you are doing. You do not need to rub shoulders with any of them because stolen money is stolen money. Such money comes in large amount. So, avoid their company or group so that you are not enticed to become a member overnight.

Avoiding envy

Everyone will get the reward of what he is doing if not instantly but in the long run. Because of this, you do not need to envy any internet scammer in your community. Even if he has built the biggest mansion in your community, it is not enough for you to be envious of him. Just lay low and stay cool. All that glitters is not gold so forget about the attractiveness.

He bought a new car of 18 million naira; and so? Is that the reason you are killing yourself? We know where the money is coming. They are eating the sweat of another man. The question is: are you ready to eat the sweat of another man? When the man has worked tirelessly by the day and sometimes part of the night, you receive his salary for him instead of him that worked for the money. That is wickedness written in capital letters.

How will you feel if someone receives the pay you suppose to receive after working for long? Will you be happy for that? If your answer is no, then let the scammers be. You have no reason to envy them because their conscience is dead. Some of them are not happy irrespective of their wealth. So, do not envy any of them in order not be tempted to join them. It is one of the capital approaches to avoid being a Yahoo boy or internet scammer. Enjoy what you legally worked for with peace of mind.

Chapter 5

Who are duped by Yahoo Boys?

It is not everyone that fall victim to the tricks of yahoo boys. There are some set of persons that are likely or have already fallen prey to these fraudsters. There are characteristics of people who fall prey to the games played by these intelligent criminals.

In this chapter of the book, we will be discussing people who are victim of internet scam masterminded by the young people in Nigeria. This is to inform the general public to be aware not to sheepishly fall to the tricks of these young gender. It covers both that of those who are victims of both local and international scams. If not informed one is deformed. Useful information is power. Those who fall prey to Yahoo boys scam are:

- The greedy

- The unexposed

- Illiterates

- The poor

- The get rich quick category

The greedy

Sometimes it sounds funny to observe how some people think. Some are very greedy and that is the reason they always fall victim to Nigeria internet fraudsters. You met an investor online and he told you that he had a project he was working on that if you can invest $5,000 in it you get your capital back with 150% interest within one month. Who does that? You are just so greedy to think the person is real.

You met someone online and he told you he has a large portion of land to sell for amount you know was much lower and you decided to send the money, you did that out of greediness. You want to harvest from where you did not plant. That is an act of greediness. The money the abroad victim sent goes to the private account of the yahoo boy.

The unexposed

Exposure is very important in the life of everyone living in this twenty first century. Always listen to things that are happening in the country. If anyone is updated and exposed to information and the trending things in the society, he is not going to be easily scammed by the Yahoo boys. Do not feel comfortable not reading news update and other information about banks.

When a bank sends notification to her customers, the customers should have time to read what the notification is all about. Some customers are too busy to read notifications from their banks. Some banks send messages concerning scam alert to their customers but many customers do not usually have the time to go through the contents of the message. That is why many fall victim. They are not exposed to useful information.

Illiterates

You will weep when you see some illiterate customers come to the bank to complain for their missing money from their accounts. Sincerely you will feel for them. The author of this book works with First Bank of Nigeria Insurance and has had personal contact with some of these men and women. They come to the bank complaining helplessly concerning their missing money from their accounts. Some of these helpless illiterate customers did not know when they disclose their secrete information to these scammers. They come to the bank looking helpless and devastated.

Sometimes, those that do not know how to read and write fall victim of fraudsters trick. Because they cannot read or write and still have accounts in the banks, they do not know when banks send scam alert messages to them. They are like people who buy cars but do not know how to drive.

There are many account holders in many banks in Nigeria that cannot read or write. These are people that the officials of banks help to fill their accounts opening forms from beginning to the end because they could not read or write. When it was the time for the illiterates to sign on the account opening forms, they thumb printed with ink and sometimes sign with their initials to complete their account opening process. They do this because they may not remember what they signed before if they use something complex.

This category of people is easily scammed by Yahoo boys. A Yahoo boy may call any of them claiming to be a customer care agent from the bank he is banking. The scammer demands for secret information which he (the illiterate) does not suppose to give out and he gives such information out freely.

At the end, the fraudster dupes the man his good amount of money because he is not educated. There are occasions where illiterates came to bank and pitiably complain how they were scammed by yahoo boys by withdrawing their money from their accounts. Some of them laid curse on the scammers on hearing that they were duped.

The Poor

Some poor people in every society are always happy to hear any news that will make them maximize their money. People of this category if they do not discipline themselves can easily fall prey to the tricks of scammers. A scammer may call them and inform them that there is an ongoing promo and if they invest a particular amount of money in their scheme, they will get 100% return within one week. Because of the fact that they are poor and want to maximize their money, they fall prey to the tricks and loss their already hard earned money.

Poverty is bad. It makes people do what they may not ordinarily do. The poor think of how to make more money. They go to the churches more hoping for miracle to happen one day and be able to meet up with the demand of the society. As a result of this, any little thing can make them fall victim in the hope that it is the miracle they have been waiting for.

For example, there was a time when scammers used to call telephone numbers at random and informed people that they won a prize in one promo. Some of these scammers called and pretended they were calling from a telecommunication company.

Some called poor MTN subscribers and told them that they won two million Nigerian naira (N2,000,000). The poor receiver of the message feels happy on getting this call that God has answered his/her prayer without knowing it was a trick. The fraudster pretending to be an agent from MTN sometimes tell the victim that for them to pay her the money she won, that she has to go and pay five thousand naira (N 5,000) to an account.

The poor woman then rushed to the bank and pay into the account details given to her to claim her money. These guys are very intelligent Nigerians; pay five thousand naira and get two million naira. The poor woman calls after the payment for her payment to be confirmed. But little did she know it was a trick.

The Yahoo boy may say that they would get back to her soon. The next is that they break the SIM card after scamming other persons with the same line. The victim calls repeatedly and she could not reach the scammer. Her hope of claiming two million naira, as miracle, she expected is gone when this happened. What a world? Poverty is bad.

The get rich quick category

So many people want to get rich quick. The get rich quick syndrome is all over the air. Some said that they do not gain anything if they do not make this money. In line with the saying, they want to make the money either by crook or by hook.

Many circular songs in Federal Republic of Nigeria are all about money. It is all about get rich quick syndrome. Some are doing a lot of dirty things because they want to make money.

It is a pity that because of this quest to get rich quick, many have fallen victim to Yahoo boys. Some have been duped by these guys because they want magic to be performed for them to make the money quick. Till today, many people who want to get rich quick are still victim of scam. It is painful but unfortunate they are trapped by their quest to get rich quick.

Chapter 6

Funny Things Yahoo Boys do

There are many things that Yahoo boys do that are funny. These Nigerian young boys abuse the masses when they do certain things. We will be looking at some of these things here. They do a lot of things that looks funny to the eyes of a rational person. They do all these things with all seriousness. To the eyes of a person that sees scam as a wrong thing, it is funny, but to someone who sees it as a games and nothing bad, those funny things are big deals. This chapter will be short but direct to the point.

Praying to God to bless their Hustle

These young criminals pray very well. Can you just imagine that? They usually pray for God to bless them in their business. A part of their prayers goes in this form "Oluwa bless my hustle. Help me to pick today". Is that not funny? The word "Oluwa" is a Yoruba word which means God. Seriously, some of these guys have lost great sense of spirituality and religion.

How can someone who scams people to enrich his pocket be praying to God to allow some people fall victim to his tricks. These guys are really crazy as the author had not seen a situation where God support evil. God is God and can never be in support of people that dupe people to make money.

They now take Christianity for levity. To them, God hears them and can make them dupe more money from people. But that is not true at all.

Giving fat offerings in the churches

The twenty first (21st) century churches are so money conscious. Some pastors in the churches of the country are ready to collect large offerings from the G boys without asking of the source of their income. Some of them who know what they do to make their money do not even care. They are after the money.

Pastors who preach about tithing every Sunday forgetting to preach about the moral lives of the congregation wait every month for fat tithes from their congregation that are into scam. Christianity is losing its value today. Materialism has taken over the stage. Pastors and priests in churches in Nigeria are more interested in prosperity than the spirituality of the congregation.

During donations in churches in Nigeria, there are different categories of people that come out to donate. The category is dependent on how much any member of the church wants to donate. These G boys are usually in First Class category. They use their ill gotten wealth to intimidate others. Pastors and priests smile and pray for them as they make their donations. It is not as if these pastors and priests do not know what these boys do to make their money but their eyes are covered with the love for money.

The G boys give fat offerings in the churches with the mindset that more doors will be opened for them to pick more money. To some of them, they do not see what they do as scam but as games through which one can make money. Because of this ideology, they parade themselves in churches without any sense of guilt.

Some of them believe that giving such huge offering from the money they stole from innocent people will make their sins forgiven. As they are in churches, their minds are filled with the next deeper actions they will take into their dirty business. It is funny that some of them leave the church and find themselves into their dirty business again after about five minutes. Some even lost concentration if the church services take much time. They look good on physical appearance but their minds are filled with evils they will commit.

It is funny. They continue to make advancement in their criminal acts and later bring some part to the church for offering. The mentality of an average Nigerian Christian is nothing to write home about. Steal from people and take some to the church. They just go to church to show people they wear expensive clothes and went him to continue with their evils.

Anyone who works will make it

To them, scam is a work. It sounds funny to see a generation of youths that strongly believe that the criminal activities they get involved in is a work. In some of their discussions, you hear that anyone who works will make it.

In the other words, anyone who keeps on digging deep and advancing in fraudulent activities will surely succeed in scamming a lot of people and make money in the long run. They say to one another "as far as you keep working hard, someone will surely pay you one day". No matter what, one client will pay one day. That is what they strongly believe.

They do not see what they do as fraud but observe it as work. Because they have this perception that they are doing work and not something bad, they put in their maximum efforts. But no matter the name they give to it, scam is scam. Fraudulent activity is a fraudulent activity anywhere in the world. They call it work to cover up. But that is really funny.

It is done to a lot of them that what they have been doing is scam and not works but scam when they find themselves in the nets of security agents in the country. Some of these young men that find themselves in the custody of Economic and Financial Crimes Commission (EFCC) discovered that what they were doing was fraud and not work as they thought. Some till today are still in many prisons in the country without knowing whether they will come out alive or not. These boys that act funny should know that what they do is not work but scam.

Chapter 7

Characteristics of Internet Scammers in Nigeria

They have features. They have the way they operate and how they live their lives as young money millionaires. Youths in Nigeria who are into internet scam have common behaviours though few persons are different but many of them share common lifestyles. They have similar approach to certain things about life. The interest in this chapter is on the

82

characteristics of Yahoo or G boys.

The characteristics of Yahoo boys are:

- Noise making

- Drug Addicts

- Womanizing

- Extravagance

- Restlessness

Noise making

G boys are noise makers. They like noisy environment. They derive joy in shouting at the top of their voices whenever they discuss in group. Their noise making attitude is a common practice they enjoy. Sometimes when people pass around them and observe them talking and shouting at the top of their voices, the people do not need a seer to tell them who they are.

When they come to banks to collect the money sent to them by their victims, their tone are high. They can shout at bank officials if directed by the officials to do certain things right. If for example the Western Union official tells the G boy that the name they gave does not match with the name in his identity card (the G boy's detail) he can get provoked and shout at the top of his voice.

It is not as if the issue cannot be resolved but he felt like making noise to show the other bank customers that he came to pick money through Western Union. Shouting is part of G boys characteristics. They are noise makers everywhere in the country. Once some of them walks into the bank to withdraw the money sent to them by their victims, the staffs know. They make some kinds of noise and that creates awareness of their presence.

When the scam that brings the money is not engineered by only one person, there may be problem while sharing of their stolen money. The proportion to be given to each may be an issue. This makes them to quarrel right there in the bank and raise dust.

Have you been to a compound where G boys are living? If you have been there you will understand what the author is writing about. Everything about them is noise. Even when they play music with their sound systems, they do that at high pitch. Even upon that, they still make noise as the music play.

Drug Addicts

Addiction is common among the youths and young fraudsters in Nigeria. It is only few G boys in the country that are free from abuse of drugs. As early as 1 A.M in the morning when they suppose to be sleeping, they are busy disturbing the people they are in the same compound with the smell of marijuana. Their lives are dependent on drugs.

Codeine and tramadol is part of them. The money they make through international and local scam get them intoxicated. This makes them behave abnormal. They combine different drugs they are not suppose to take just because they want to get high and feel happy.

Because of the drugs these youths abuse, they have the mind of doing what a person cannot ordinarily do. They dupe both the young and old without thinking of the repercussions of what they did. They do not think of tomorrow and are not moved of their evil deeds. They see evil as normal and what everyone has to do to survive. They say that every way is way.

A man who is in his right sense cannot just pick a knife, cut out the tong, the genital, eye, and breast of a lady all because of money. They become high before they can do that. They get high because they do not want to have any sign of mercy toward the victim. It is really sad.

Fraudsters are drug abusers. They get high and feel as if they are on top. They talk from one angle to another. They narrate stories on how they were able to dupe their victims' huge amounts of money. They indirectly damage their livers by drugs. If internet scammers can reduce hands on how they consume drugs, their atrocities will reduce. Drugs which they take reduce them to lower animals.

Do you know some of these young men who are into drugs today are victims of sexual transmitted diseases? Some of them are victims of Human Immune Virus (HIV) because they had unprotected sex when they were high in drugs. They find out that they suffer from AIDS when they go for test after long time sickness. Drug abuse is bad. It can make ones sense of how to do things right reduced.

Alcoholism for instance can have negative effect when it comes to reproduction. It can make a man impotent. It destroys some useful chemicals needed for impregnating a woman. But little do these drug abusers know about it. They drug themselves without understanding the adverse effects of what they are doing. There are problems in some homes today. What is the cause of the issue? Difficulty in child bearing is the reason for that.

Womanizing

Money intoxicates people. When someone makes money he could not believe he would make in his lifetime, such money can intoxicate him. He made the money through scam and it is so much. Before you know what is happening, he begins to misbehave high-time because he is intoxicated with what he has.

Today, you see him in a party with set of women and tomorrow you see him with another set of women. He continues that way all through his living as a youth. The money is there and that is why you see him doing all sorts of rubbish without rethink. He makes the money through fraudulent ways and hence lost sense of value of money.

But the trick is that some of these ladies they carry around do not know that their lives are in danger by doing what they are doing. Some of them have been used for ritual by the G boys unknown to them to make more money. They pretend to love the ladies but they do not know that something has been collected from their bodies by these wicked guys to make more money and grow richer. Some G guys are very diabolic but in coded way.

Some of them after sleeping with the women they carry to parties use handkerchief to clean the virginal fluid from the women and later take it to fetish experts that do ritual for them. The women sometimes remain barren forever or face nemeses all through their lives. They have ways they operate to use women for their diabolic rituals.

The one that happened recently in Shoprite, Warri, in Delta state of Nigeria made a lot of ladies live in fear. It taught them lesson that not all G boys they see on the street are nice. Some of them are devils wearing human skin. They are heartless and they are everywhere. It taught the ladies lesson that not every guy that dress in clean clothes and drive good cars are safe to follow.

That one that happened in Warri on November 2018 is an example. The victim met a guy in Shoprite who offered her N50,000 (fifty thousand naira) just to stick a finger in her vagina in the restroom of the supermarket. Little did she know that the Yahoo guy had interior motive. Immediately the guy sent N50,000 to her bank account she agreed without asking the boy any questions and went straight with him to the toilet. She came out with the guy after both of them spent about 15mins in the toilet feeling excited. After she escorted the guy to his car she went to her friend rejoicing (Cyril Okonkwo 2018).

After about 30 minutes of the G boy leaving the area, the lady who was fingered began to feel the urge to urinate. She then ran into toilet and began to urinate blood. She ran out of the toilet shouting at the top of her voice but the blood kept coming out of her virginal. It was dawn on her at that point that the guy that fingered her just used her for ritual for fifty thousand Nigerian naira only. She bled to death at Shoprite Warri. If you are a single lady and a Yahoo boy woo you, say no to him. Many of them are okay at doing evil because of their high quest for money.

Extravagance

They live extravagantly. It is part of them as they have their ill gotten wealth with them to always spend. They feel as if it is nothing and to some of them is nothing for sure. A situation whereby their clients send much money to them, they have much to spend extravagantly. Some of the yahoo boys are young and because of that lack the experience of what to do with money.

They go to parties and buy expensive wines and pour them on the ground. They pour the content of the bottles of wine on the ground to show the people that they have plenty of money. They have money they duped from innocent people to waste in parties. Some of them after pouring the wines on the ground decide to drink later. They are intoxicated with money made through fraudulent ways.

They enter supermarkets in the country and buy a lot of expensive items. They are indeed expensive and ladies who could not hold themselves are attracted by them. Some of them when in the supermarkets after buying the items may not even use them for a long time.

Some even give items they bought to use to other persons. This is after the items have stay in their houses for a long time and they feel they cannot use them again. G boys are married to extravagant lifestyle. They behave quite boldly, prove their social status in the online space and sometimes neglect the moral norms typical for ordinary Nigerian citizens. Yahoo boys publish photos of their expensive watches, cars and clothes. They show off.

Restlessness

So many Yahoo boys in the Federal Republic of Nigeria are restless. They are always afraid of their living. They do not know anything that may happen in the nearest minutes. Even when they are in social gathering, their eyes go to many places within few minutes. They are afraid of the evil they committed sometime ago coming after them.

When they are in their rooms and someone knocks on their doors, it takes them time to come and open the door. They are afraid because they do not know if the person knocking on the door is a police officer. Some are restless because they do not know if the person knocking comes with other people hiding somewhere. They may be attacked by armed robbers when they open the doors without proper observation. They are fraudsters and therefore live like criminals which they are.

There is no peace for the wicked. Because they are wicked by duping both the poor, the old, the rich and the illiterates to enrich their own pockets, they would never have peace. Some who kill to renew their diabolic powers and make them active again are living in fear. Their minds fly anytime they see the Corps or police officers. The reason is because they do not know if the evil they did have been discovered. Their hands are not clean so they are afraid.

Because of their evil deeds, some are restless when stopped at checkpoints by police. They are restless when police officers ask for their mobile phones to see what they have in it including their photo gallery section. The G boys may not like to hand their phones over because of the scam documents they may have inside.

Chapter 8

How Yahoo Boys have Influenced Nigerian Security

It is a pity that those that are employed and established to shun crime are sleeping. They are like sleeping lions that cannot do anything good. They failed in their duties and cannot make any impact to make effective changes.

Policemen in Nigeria have familiarized themselves with these young scammers in Nigeria to the extent that they cannot talk to them as police officers. Instead of these officers to do their job by searching these young men and then charging them to Law court if found guilty, they are busy praising them when they drive pass police check points or even in police stations. It is a shame to Nigerian Police force in general.

Some policemen instead of arresting these G boys for defrauding innocent people are interested in collecting money from them at different strategic points. Those who are assigned in banks to secure the banks help left their fundamental duties and stand patiently at the gates of the banks waiting for any yahoo boy that comes out of the bank to beg for money. They are always eager to fill their pockets with money to be given to them by yahoo boys everyday. They lost sense of what they are sent to the bank to do.

Nigeria police officers have turned themselves to nothing because of the influence of these internet fraudsters in the country. Sometimes once these young fraudsters offer bribes to them while driving their cars and stopped at checkpoints, the policemen on duty allow them to pass.

They did not bother to check to find out if the yahoo boys are carrying exhibit in their cars. Some yahoo boys who kidnapped for ritual have passed police checkpoints freely because they influenced the officers with their ill gotten wealth.

Some yahoo boys who were arrested for one offence or the other are set free without adequate punishment because they influenced the members of the force with their money. Once they pay mouth watering amount of money to the top officials, they are set free. The case is closed and no need for further investigation on the case that makes them find themselves in the sale. That is the attitude of some of the security officers we have in Nigeria. They allow themselves to be easily influenced by the young fraudsters in the society.

Instead of standing for justice, they stand for what is evil. They have failed both the government and the citizens of the country. Many yahoo boys are not even afraid of police again. Some of them challenge policemen at checkpoints for doing their duty. In European countries, fraudsters have no say but the reverse is the case in Nigeria.

In United States of America for instance, fraudsters tremble on seeing police but it is not so in Nigeria. Over there, they hide on seeing the officers on duty. But in Nigeria, fraudsters feel no atom of fear on seeing police officers. They know that if it becomes tough, they bribe them with money and then go their way. In United States, attempt to bribe a police officer is a capital offence but it is normal in Nigeria. Your money can buy you out in the country even when you committed a criminal act.

Chapter 9

Why Many Nigerian Youths are Fraudsters (Causes)

Something does not just happen for happening sake. There are things that cause something to happen. There are some factors that make many Nigerians find themselves in that state today. It is a national issue. In this section of the book, we will be digging deep on the causes of Nigerian youths' involvement in fraudulent activities to make money for a living. The causes of Nigerian youths involvement in scam, hence called yahoo or G boys are as follow:

- High youth unemployment

- Poor moral training by parents and guardians

- High quest for riches

- Insatiability of Nigerian youths

High youth unemployment

Youth unemployment is the mother of many issues that youths all over the country have been facing for a long time now. It is a big challenge and has fuelled the involvement of many Nigerians into scams of various kinds. The belief If you cannot beat them you join them is what they decided to go into after searching for jobs for long time and could not get any.

Some of the youths may not like to find themselves into the

attitude of scamming other people for money. But they became interested in the dirty game after being at home for a long time without finding any reasonable job. To keep life going and also to meet the demand of the society, they go into scam.

Initially, they might have structured their minds that nothing will make them to be yahoo boys of any form. They believed in themselves that they can make it on their own without soiling their hands into any form of dirty practices in the name of making money. As time goes on, they see their mates whom they know they were far better than then in school driving expensive cars and "doing things" in the town. The young men approach them whom are doing well in the society and to their surprise they are into fraud of different kinds both local and international.

After engaging the G boys in discussion to know the way forward as they who were waiting for jobs could not find any, they are trained into scam by their mates. They start doing fraud in the name of yahoo as they grow in level in the dirty business. Sometimes their conscience judge them but they moved on as they convince themselves that the reason for them doing what they do is because there is no job in the country. They continued to advance in scam in the country while the citizens who are not into scam tremble in fear not to fall victim.

Poor moral training by parents and guardians

So many authors that write in many genres were trained by their parents on how to do things and do them right. The author of the book you are reading right now is able to maintain certain standards in his life because he was well trained by his parents as well. He grew with the teaching to always do what is right and avoid doing what is wrong till he found himself into the field of writing on youth topics from his university days till date. It is a good one and moral practice was instilled into him right from when he was little.

The reason why many young people in Nigeria both the ladies and the guys are into fraud is due to the fact that they lack good moral training by their parents. They are poor when it comes to the area of doing things in ways that are morally acceptable. That is the reason why there is high moral decay in Nigeria today.

The youths want to make the money anyhow. They do not care to know if the channel they will use to make the money is dirty or not. It is all about making money. "If I do not make this money wetin I gain". That is the slogan of many Nigeria youths and it has been pushing them to do a lot of atrocities just to make money. It is sad that some of them do not know they will regret their ill actions latter in life.

A youth who is trained morally by the parents will not have the mind to kill a fellow human for ritual in the sense that he wants to fortify his diabolic power to be able to scam more clients for money. The fetish power of Yahoo boys came to be because many of them are very poor in terms of morality. According to Samson Ezea of The Guardian newspaper, "Yahoo boys don't have morality. They usually stop at nothing to deceive people and pocket their money (Samson Ezea 2017)".

Any person that comes from a good family where morality is practiced and cannot be done without understands the value of life. To such person, no amount of hunger for money can make him to kill. Life is sacred and should not be gambled with. Such person understands that no amount of wealth can be exchanged with human life. Whether the activities of these wicked men that kill for ritual is called Yahoo plus or not, poor moral integration is one of the reasons why they misbehave. Parents should take it as a point of duty to train their children on how to live moral lives to reduce the menace of fraudulent activities among the youths in the country.

High quest for riches

Our youths are getting mad for riches. Some of them can do anything for riches. They see the teaching of waiting for their own time to shine as old fashioned story. They want their riches today without waste of time of any kind. They want to wear expensive clothes, buy expensive houses and cars. They want to be praised by people. They always desire to command respect because of riches.

Because of the quest to possess such attributes, they go extra miles to get riches. If duping people can bring the wealth they want, they can do that without considering who is affected negatively. They do not care about who gets hurt in their quest to get rich quick. The attitude of high quest for riches has made our youths hide their faces in shame while doing what they cannot do ordinarily to make money when in their right senses.

"Yet, the cause of Cyber-crime in Nigeria as inordinate desire for wealth, you will find that a large gap exists between the rich and the rest of the population in Nigeria. Consequently, many attempt to level up using the fastest means possible. For any business to succeed, return on investment needs to be growing at a geometric rate with a minimal risk. Cyber crimes require little investment in time and money in addition to a conducive environment. Nigeria offers such environment and many cyber criminals take advantage of that (Kubiat Umana 2018)".

Insatiability of Nigerian youths

The word insatiability means impossible to satiate or satisfy. You have two cars yet you want to have ten with hundred houses. The more some Nigerian youths have, the more they want to have. Many of them are never filled. They are like oceans and hence want to be oceanic bank. Even Oceanic bank at a point liquidated and later joined Access Bank of Nigeria because they do not have enough capitals mandated them by the Central Bank of Nigeria. So no matter how much a Nigerian youth want to acquire, he can collapse one day if he or she does not take it easy. Fraud is not a good and no amount of baptism can prevent it from being what it is.

It is not as if it is a bad thing to desire for more but it becomes bad when one takes advantage of other persons because he wants to grow. That is wickedness and wrong perception on how to acquire wealth. There are people that have acquired many wealth today and they got them genuinely. So why dupe other persons because you want to make money?

If you desire to go higher in life, it is good and never a bad one. But do not do that at the expense of other persons that are working hard to make living. Imagine a situation why Nigerian Yahoo boy scams an advanced woman of hundred thousand naira and it took the woman about three months to save the money from the little trade she does in a rural area of one timid village. The Yahoo boy becomes happy for succeeding in the scam and the woman cries out for been a victim.

Insatiability is bad. Do not be envious of any person because you want to acquire what the person has. Be contented with what you have at your current level in life. It is time for our Nigerian youths to understand that no one will carry wealth to the grave. Let us be happy with what we have today and make genuine efforts for a brighter tomorrow.

Chapter 10

Why Nigerian Government is not serious with the fight against Internet Fraudsters

We all know the truth. We know what is going on and fully understand why the government of the Federal Republic of Nigeria behaves as if they do not see anything wrong with the activities of the young scammers in the country. The government officials pretend as if they are doing something to stop the activities of Yahoo boys in the currently but critical examination will make you find out that they, the government, are not serious with the fight against these criminals in the country. They have their aims for doing that.

High youth unemployment

Due to high youth unemployment in the country, many Nigerian youths find solace in internet scam to make money illegally and continue living. Many have really made money through this means and are really living large irrespective of the fact that the money is made through criminal act. But the government themselves sometimes see it as a game the way the G guys see it as a game and the way to make money by playing on the intelligence of their English abroad lovers. Their perception on what they do to make their money is totally different from that of the person who believes that moral lifestyle should be the priority.

Some Yahoo boys receive dollars from their abroad lovers every month. Because they have really worked on their women abroad lovers and seriously worked on their emotions as well, their lovers send money to them down to Nigeria anytime they are paid in their work places over there. In fact, some of the scammers who claimed to really be in love with their lovers in Europe and America receive up to 40% of their women's salary every month. Once the abroad woman is paid her salary in a month, she sends the 40% of her lover down to Nigeria. She does this because she (the American lover) will not like to lose her lover to another woman. In her thinking, her Nigerian lover will come over and marry her one day.

Due to the trick of this kind, the fraudsters make a lot of money. Many of them make much more money than those who do legal jobs in Nigeria. That is the reason why many of them live extravagant lifestyles. They buy houses and buy expensive cars. They make money from their lovers that live and work in abroad.

Because the woman an internet scammer claims to love lives in abroad, they can have as many lovers as possible. Their communications are at distance and therefore communicate through the internet. The Yahoo boys take it as business while the white women believe that they have real lovers that will one day come over and live with them.

A situation whereby a Yahoo boy has five white women that pays him about $700 (seven hundred dollars) each every month, what is the need to search for Nigerian job again? When the $700 is multiplied by 5, it gives a total of $3,500 (three thousand five hundred dollars). The Nigeria equivalent of $3,500 is N1, 260, 000 (one million two hundred and sixty thousand naira). How many Nigeria jobs can give you such pay in a month? It is very hard to get unless top staffs in oil companies in the country. That amount of money is some workers four years salary in Nigeria.

The reason for the analysis is to show you why Nigerian government is not serious with the fight against internet scammers in Nigeria. Due to high youth unemployment in the country which the government have failed to tackle, the government sees the engagement of young men and women in the country into scam as means through which they employ themselves. That is called self employment. Because of this, the pressure mounted on the government by the youth as a result of job scarcity has reduced. The government pretends as if they fight these internet scammers but they do not really do that.

How many jobs will they provide for the hungry youths if they succeed in stopping them totally? This is what goes on in the mind of government officers in the country. They feel reluctant about the fight against internet scammers in the country and yet showcase to the world that they are doing something to stop the Yahoo boys in the country.

Reduction in physical robbery attack and other local crimes

Because Nigerian young internet fraudster are busy with their activities of extorting money from foreign men and women through their tricks, the attacks on citizens of the country physically has reduced. The behaviour of young men in the country moving into homes and injuring the victims because they refused to give what they demanded has reduced drastically. Some of these young men sometimes kill the people they attacked if they refuse to give the money they demand.

But with the emergence of internet scam among the youths of the country, the young men are busy working on white people for money. This has shifted their attention from attacking people physically because of money. The government of the country feels that because of the opportunity provided to internet scammers, they have little to worry about.

Before now, politicians are very afraid while travelling and driving around the country. Their fear is usually because of attack on them by G boys in the country. Since Yahoo boys began to dig deeper and make their money through dirty ways, the government fears less than former. Reason is because the 419 (the scammers) make more money and they do not focus on them (the politicians) again.

Kidnapping was on the rise before. The youths of the country sometimes target men who are well to do including the politicians. They believed that a huge ransom has the tendency of changing their lives to better. Sometimes it take them much time before they are able to secure and executive their plans effectively. Since some of these men are now into scams of different levels, the rate at which physical attack of this kind in the country is brought low. The young men and women have found another source of livelihood to them which is stealing from people who are financially buoyant through the internet.

Poverty reduction among young fraudsters

A young man who can buy a car of nine million naira (N9, 000, 000) is not a poor person. Irrespective of the wicked tricks these young Nigerian scammers apply to make their money, they are rich people. Some of them send fishing messages to the email addresses of their suspects and ended up getting the details of the people they target once the victims click on any of the links and register for one thing or the other. That is why it is not advisable to click on the links that are inside the massages of your junk or spam box.

Many of these young criminals in Nigeria are building houses in different parts of the country and the Nigerian government is aware that some of the money they used to raise the structures are made through scam and yet could not do anything to bring them to book. They cannot act to stop the criminal activities of these young people because they, the government, know that the reason why these boys are into fraud is because they failed to provide enough jobs for them. Because of job scarcity in the country, the boys jumped into scam to make money and get alleviated from poverty.

But in general, that does not justify what they do as being right. Scam is scam but Nigerian government does not want to come out openly to fight the Yahoo boys because they know they have failed the youths of the country. They the youths do not want to continue to be in their state of poverty and therefore are making money either by hook or by crook.

How Nigerian government can take down Yahoo Boys (fraudsters) if they are serious

If Nigerian government is sincere to themselves and really wants to deal with the internet scammers in the Federal Republic of Nigeria, there are simple approaches they can apply to get the job done. There are things they have to do to break the wings of these young men and women that are giving the country bad name abroad and even within. They will stop their operations if they enforce the ideas to be discussed.

EFCC partnering with local banks

That is one of the capital approaches to adopt. The government of the country Nigeria need to charge this group to up their games. Economic and Financial Crimes Commission really needs to meet all local banks and discuss with them on how to get these guys down. But on the other hand, banks may not be open to accept the proposals of EFCC to get any of the Yahoo boys down.

Do you know the reason behind that? The reason is because staffs of the commercial banks in the country are friends to many young fraudsters in the country. They have familiarized themselves with these boys to the extent that they are good friends. Even the managers of some local banks in the country strike deals with the Yahoo boys before they are allowed to receive the money sent to them from abroad by their lovers or any person they scammed. Before these boys are allowed to receive the money sent to them if it is much, they see the manager first to know how much they will give to him after the money is pulled through Western Union. It is a hidden corruption that goes on in banks all over the country.

But we cannot continue like this. A crime is a crime and the government of the country in her power have to put a stop to it. The EFCC should not allow themselves to be influence by these small boys that are giving the country bad names. They have painted the image of this country black. The government has to send EFCC agents to banks to work as undercovers among the staffs of the banks. Whenever the G boys come to the bank to catch the money sent to them through Western Union or Money Grams, they undercover should send signals to the nearest EFCC branch in that location.

When the team arrives, they interrogate the suspects to find out who they are. After that, they arrest these boys and take them to the appropriate places where they will face trials. This will help in a long way to stop the operation of the fraudsters to minimal level. Proper enforcement will yield positive results.

By the time these boys are arrested and face trials for some times, they will begin to adjust. At that point they will find out that what they have been doing is not game but a total criminal act. Bank should always supply information to Economic and Financial Crimes Commission to always get these boys that are messing up the country down.

Working with Police

It is true that the security sector of Nigeria has been infected by Yahoo boys in the country because they give money freely to the security men and women in the country which turns out to be bribe. Bribery and corruption is one of the major challenges in Nigeria and it has robbed the citizens of the country to a very great extent.

To achieve a good result in the fight against internet scammers in a particular region of the country, strategic ideas need to be applied. Because the police officers in a particular community have familiarized themselves with the scammers, the first step is to transfer all the police officers in the areas where these fraudsters have their operations. The transfer will give room to bring in new officers that will work effectively without looking and the faces of the scammers. The transfer is to come as order from the government of the country.

Before the new officers arrive in their new areas of operation, they are educated on what they are going to the new area to do. They will also be taught on the techniques they will apply to track down the internet scammers. It will make their works in the new easier.

One of the ways to identify internet scammers in Nigeria is through the pictures they have in the image galleries of their phones. It is common with those that defraud white people through dating sites. They usually have nude pictures of their own or that of the person they impersonate. They have these pictures so that they can arouse their victims emotionally and get reasonable amount of money from them.

The police officers with the power of the government will be allowed to go through the phones of the suspected Yahoo boys. Any picture that has resemblance with that created by internet fraudsters will have the owner of the phone interrogated and tried by law if he is detected to be a G boy.

Also, the police will be mandated to visit hostels and homes in those areas. With this monitoring, students' internet fraudsters will reduce their dirty operations. Visitation by the special squad will make many student fraudsters quit from being scammers. It is a great idea that will reduce internet scam in the country. By the time many are arrested and punished for their fraudulent activities, others will learn their lesson. The punishment for internet fraud or

123

scam includes spending years in prisons.

Chapter 11

The Insiders, VPN use, and Ponzi Scheme Promoters

This topic is a crucial one. In this chapter, we will be discussing about the insiders that work with young fraudsters from Nigeria. These insiders are into "business" with fraudsters from Nigeria. The do their "business" together and share profit at the end of the transaction. And some insiders also help these fraudsters with the claim that they are in love with them.

If you are an American, you will be surprised at what goes on in your country with the fraudsters. If you are from Canada,

Germany, United Kingdom and France, or other European countries, the same thing happens. The shocking truth is that some of your citizens help Nigerian fraudsters to defraud your own people. They are the insiders Yahoo boys have in your country.

Do you know what VPN is? What function does it perform? How does it help Yahoo boys from Nigeria achieve their aim in the dirty jobs they perform from Nigeria? The acronym VPN means virtual private network. I will answer the other questions under a subheading.

Young fraudsters from Nigeria have promoted many ponzi schemes on the web. Some of them do this both online and offline. They promise their victims high interest rate if they can invest in their companies.

They interest are not realistic and yet greedy foreigners and local persons still fall to them. I will tell you what happened to the people later. The information is yet to be unfolded fully.

The Insiders

These are the people who reside in foreign countries that help young fraudsters from Nigeria achieve their scam successfully. They help them in executing their tasks to the end. They make

Yahoo boys collect enough cash they need from their clients which would not have been possible without they the insiders.

Some Yahoo boys make some foreign women fall in love with them in the course of their dirty business. They met some women on social media site like Facebook. From there they began to talk. Gradually they built intimacy with each other. At this point, it is hard for a day to pass without the two having video call to see each other.

Some of these women that fall in love with them are easily aroused asexually. They are usually older than the male young fraudsters. Also, some are women that divorced their husbands and are searching for new love. They fall cheap to these Nigerian young men.

In they course of them being in love with each other, the two would not mind going nude when they are video calling. That is one of the ways they show their love to each other. The victim, who is the foreign woman, goes to bed all night thinking about the young man. Emotional attachment can begin to set in.

Something strong starts happening between the two. Sometimes Yahoo boys go for penis enlargement just to "blow" the mind of their foreign women lovers when they go naked on online video calls.

Sexting is their thing when they are not on video calls. Sexting is sending, receiving, or forwarding sexually explicit messages, photographs, or images, primarily between mobile phones, of oneself to others. They send some erotically amplified messages to each other but the weight of the one constructed by the young fraudsters is higher. This is because they want to get the women fully involved and believe whatever thing they tell them. They don't just want to scam money out of the women but they want to convert them to insiders in future.

I don't care

I will

And you'll scream and squirt everywhere

I want your big hard dick inside of me

Where it's nice and wet waiting for you

I'll tie you up to the bed and get on top of you after eating you out and be so rough and passionate, you'll be itching to get out of those handcuffs so you can ride me till kingdom cum

God I hope you're hard right now

  iMessage 

    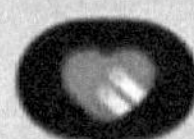  

The conversion showing sexting between Nigerian young fraudster and the foreign woman lover

When the conversion between Nigerian young fraudsters and the foreign American and European women become stronger and they fall in love, the women are used as insiders by the fraudsters.

How Nigerian Young Fraudsters use Americans and Europeans as Insiders

Some American women have been agents through which their people get scammed by Nigerian young fraudsters. You can read that sentence again. That is true. They foolishly follow the instruction of these fraudsters all because they are in love.

There had been occasions American women helped receive money for Nigerian fraudsters and then sent the money to them in Nigeria. That is the scenario we will discuss here. That will tell you how the insiders work.

Sometimes these internet fraudsters dupe Americans and the victims need American accounts numbers to pay in the money they were instructed to pay because of the product or services the fraudsters claimed they sell. And the fraudsters did not have

American account numbers even though they pretend to be Americans.

To get the money, they called or chatted up their loyal American women online. They usually lied to them that they sold something to an American and the person wants to pay to American account numbers but they do not have any. So, they appealed to their women and they sent their American account numbers to them.

The victim sent the money to the account expecting the service or the product delivered to him. As soon as the money entered the account of the American lovers, they sent the money to the Nigerian lover through Western Union or other international transaction mean.

The women ended up making scamming of their people easy. As soon as the Nigerian fraudster got his money, he may tell the victim that his commodity will soon be delivered to him. After some time, he blocked any avenue the victim may use to reach him again. At that point, the money had gone and it can be thousands of dollars.

This same thing happens in other European countries. They use their women to complete their tasks. European women are used to achieve their tasks. At a point when these women understand what their so called Nigerian lovers are doing, they demand their own cut of the money any time each deal is completed.

VPN use by Online Fraudsters from Nigeria

As technology is growing, things are changing. Some of these changes can be positive but at the same time can be negative as well. G boys have been using VPN to change their location and scam foreigners of good amount of dollars. That is the negative use of VPN. In Nigeria, young internet fraudsters don't easily let another person handle their phones because they do not want anyone to tamper with the "wicked" software and location settings that run in their mobile phones.

Virtual Private Network (VPN) can be free and some can be bought from software developing companies. A VPN is created by establishing a virtual point-to-point connection through the use of dedicated circuits or with tunneling protocols over existing networks. It has helped the dirty job of Yahoo boys from Nigeria.

A Yahoo boy can be in Nigeria and his location shows New York, United States of America because he set his VPN to that location.

So you can be in United States online while you know your real location in one timid community in Nigeria. When people from US check their IP address, they see United States IP address. VPN makes it possible.

A fraudster can pretend to be in United State and want to hook up with someone online. He may engage a man into discussion on a dating site online. He uses an identity of woman while he chats with the man from Arizona, United States. When their discussion gets romantically strong, the man may appeal to see "her". To the man, the "lady" in question is in United State because the IP address shows that. But little does he know that the "lady" is not in the same country with him but VPN made it possible.

He fixes a date with the "lady" and two days to the day of the date, the "lady" appeals to the man to please send her some dollars for transport and to get a good cloth for the date. "She" may claim to be a final year student and ran out of money. Because the man is already in love and feeling something for the "lady", he sends some dollars to the PayPal account of the scammer.

The man will not know that the "lady" he has been chatting with is a man in the real world. He just uses another person's picture on dating site and plays the role of a lady. After receiving the money, he (the fraudster impersonating to be a lady) blocks the man. The man will not be able to reach her again. But some fraudsters may continue to play more games with the man to extort more money from him.

Ponzi Schemes Promoters

Young fraudsters from Nigeria promote Ponzi schemes. This comes in various ways. They construct means through which they succeed in taking people's money through this. They carry out this task through Facebook, Instagram, Twitter, and other platforms. They even build fake websites just to still from people and the sites expire after few months when they are done stealing from a group of people.

With the cryptocurrency market being so volatile, it's not uncommon to hear about massive gains over a short period of time. This makes classic pyramid or Ponzi schemes an easier sell to investors as people are less likely to view them as "too good to be true." Austrian investment scheme Optiment promised a whopping 4% weekly return to some investors and ended up reportedly stealing more than 12,000 bitcoins.

Many people have lost their money in Ponzi schemes managed by

Nigerian fraudsters. They may tell you that you will get double your invested money in 45 minutes. Which kind of business gives that kind of return in real market? Do not listen to them and do not fall victim.

Some of them can hack the Facebook accounts of your friends on that social media site. They impersonate that your Facebook friend and begin to send out messages that are Ponzi in construction. Even if you know that you social media friend too well, do not send any money to the account you are instructed to send money to. You should see her first. Some of these fraudsters even hack the phone numbers of social media users.

I have received countless of Ponzi messages in my Facebook Messenger inbox from these fraudsters. They hacked the Facebook accounts of my friends and then sent the Ponzi scheme messages to me. They failed because am informed in terms of security. See my conversation with him below.

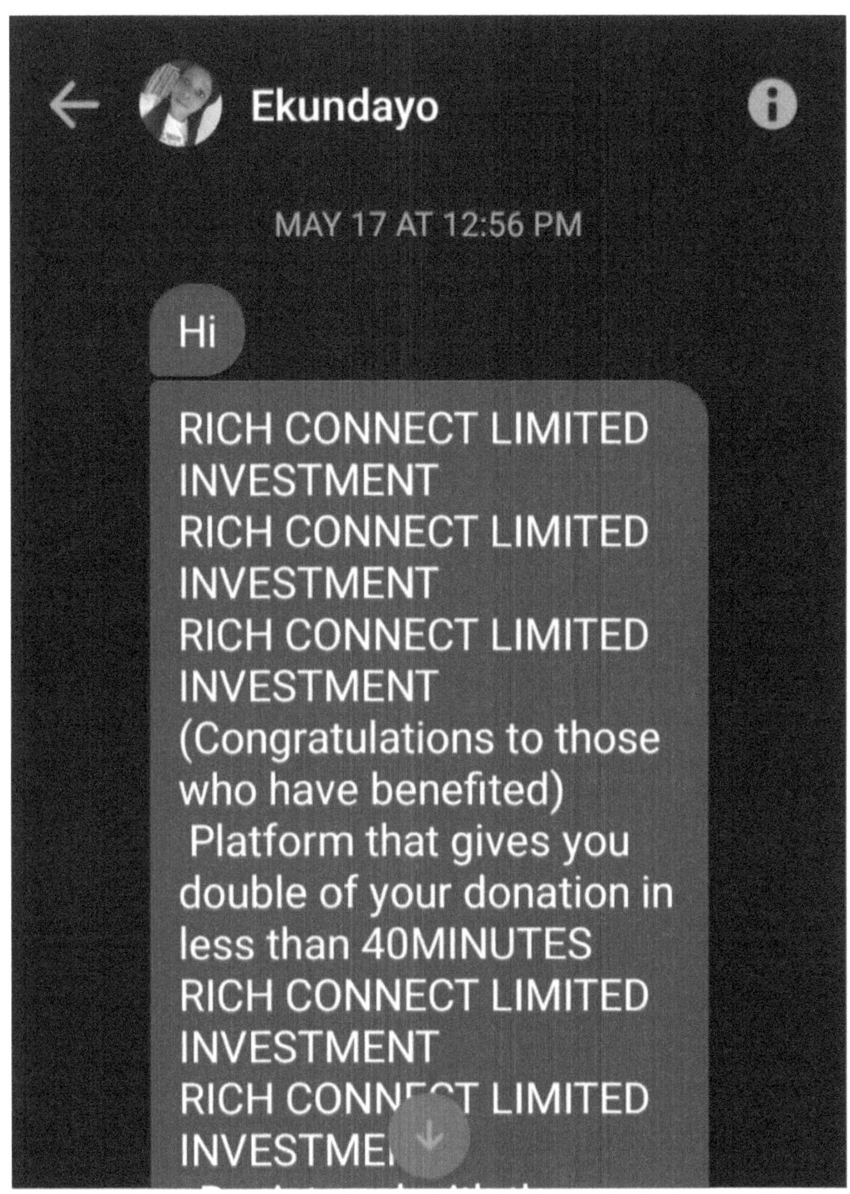

Ekundayo
MAY 17 AT 12:56 PM
Hi
RICH CONNECT LIMITED INVESTMENT
RICH CONNECT LIMITED INVESTMENT
RICH CONNECT LIMITED INVESTMENT
(Congratulations to those who have benefited)
Platform that gives you double of your donation in less than 40MINUTES
RICH CONNECT LIMITED INVESTMENT
RICH CONNECT LIMITED INVESTME

Ekundayo
RICH CONNECT LIMITED INVESTMENT
RICH CONNECT LIMITED INVESTMENT
Registered with the Corporate Affairs Commission of Nigeria.

CAC No 036463.
PACKAGES AVAILABLE
10K TO GET 20K
15K TO GET 30K
20K TO GET 40K
25K TO GET 50K
30K TO GET 60K
40K TO GET 80K
35K TO GET 70K
50K TO GET 100K
55K TO GET 110K

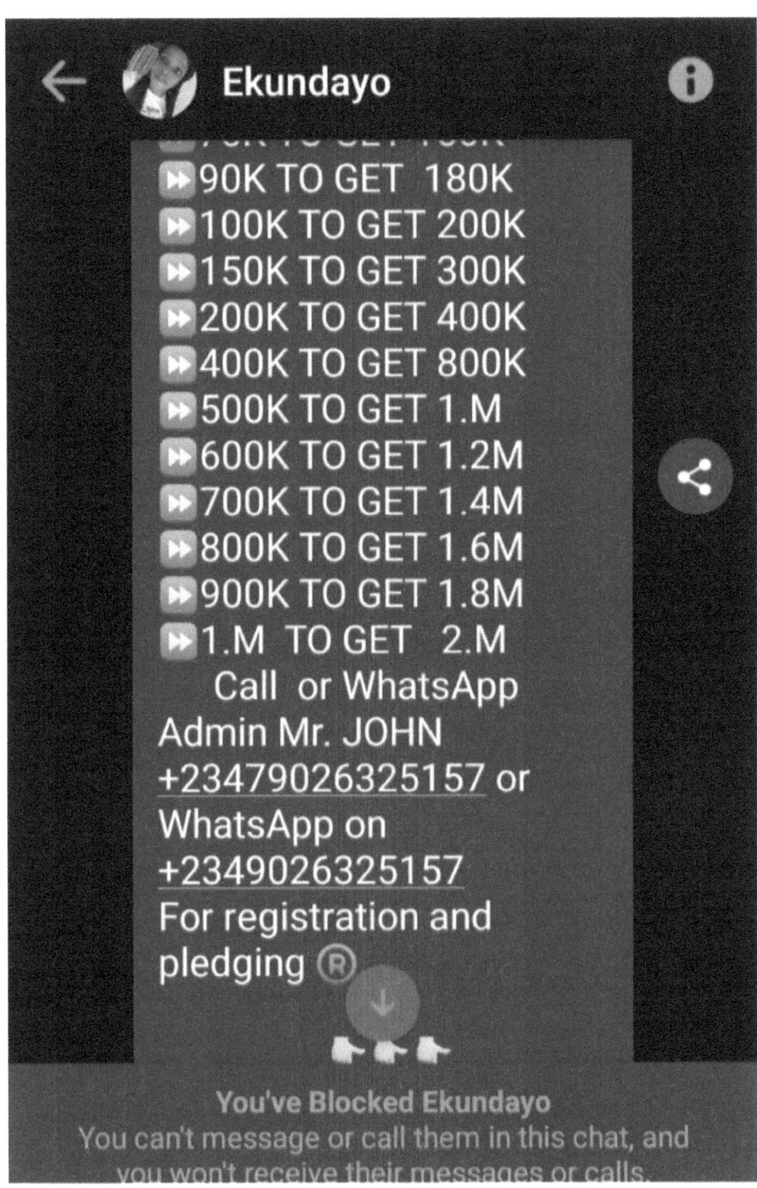
Ekundayo
90K TO GET 180K
100K TO GET 200K
150K TO GET 300K
200K TO GET 400K
400K TO GET 800K
500K TO GET 1.M
600K TO GET 1.2M
700K TO GET 1.4M
800K TO GET 1.6M
900K TO GET 1.8M
1.M TO GET 2.M
Call or WhatsApp
Admin Mr. JOHN
+23479026325157 or
WhatsApp on
+2349026325157
For registration and
pledging ®
You've Blocked Ekundayo
You can't message or call them in this chat, and
you won't receive their messages or calls.

After I told the impersonator that he is a scammer, he argued that he is for real and they pay within 45 minutes. The next step I took was to report his account and blocked him on Messenger App.

I advices you use strong password for your Facebook account. Also do two steps verification in your account to avoid any form of hacking of your Facebook account.

References

- Adunni .A. (2018), Alleged Yahoo guy dupes Oyinbo woman he met on Badoo N81m, check out what she did to him in Warri, published by Legit News, Nigeria

- Ahamefuna (2017), 2 Yahoo Boys Sell Lagos Lagoon To American Based Business Man For N787million, published by Nairaland, Nigeria

- Cyril .O. (2018), Yahoo Boy fingers Girl to Death in Warri Shoprite, published by Shoolsbiz Students Hot Joint, Nigeria

- Don Silas (2018), Fr. Mbaka exposes his impersonator before his congregation [VIDEO], published by Daily Post news company, Nigeria

- Federal Bureau of Investigation (2017), Binary Options Fraud, Published by Federal Bureau of Investigation, United States of America

- Kubiat .U. (2018), Causes of Cyber Crime in Nigeria, published by Research Cyber, Nigeria

- Lawrence .P. (2018), Avoiding Scams How To Protect Your Money, published by Commodity LLC, 1013 Centre Road, Suite 403S, Wilmington, New Castle, Delaware, 19805, United States

- Madaily Gist (2018), Top 10 Wealthiest Yahoo Boys and their Luxury LifeStyles (PHOTOS), published by Ma Daily Gist, Nigeria

- Oluwaseun .A. & Ruth .O.(2018), Ex-deputy governor's daughter allegedly used for money rituals by boyfriend, published by The Guardian News, Nigeria

- Osayimwen .O. G. (2018), The Celebrity Status of Yahoo Boys in Nigeria, published by Information Nigeria, Nigeria

- Perez .B. (2018), Corpse of missing DELSU student found without breast, tongue, published by Vanguard News, Nigeria

- Samson .E. (2017), Prevalence of Internet Fraud among Nigerian Youths, published by The Guardian News, Nigeria

About the Author

Okwuagbala Uzochukwu Mike P acquired his first degree in Metallurgical and Material Engineering, went through training on networking organized by Cisco Certified Network Associate (CCNA), and certified by the College of Insurance and Financial Management as a professional insurance agent in Nigeria. He is also a website designer, mentor to young people and youth motivator.

He once taught young Nigerians in secondary school. He is passionate to acquire new skills and that is why he reads and makes research to acquire unique skills in different areas of life. Currently, Uzochukwu Mike works as financial advisor in First Bank of Nigerian Insurance. He derives joy in writing helpful non-fiction books and articles.

Uzochukwu Mike has written over thirteen books that sale both locally and internationally. Also, he has written as contributor to powerful books which involve great scholars as co-contributors. Example of the book that he contributed as a chapter author is "WE THE PEOPLE: Building A New Democracy in Nigeria As A Model for Africa". The book is a product of a fine team of 18 distinguished authors who live in four different countries of the world; Nigeria, the United States of America, Britain and France.

Some of the books he has written on youths are: Basic Information in Youth and Youth Empowerment, Types of Youth Empowerment, Importance of Youth Empowerment, Youth Unemployment: Statistics and Causes, Guide to Youth Challenges, and Tips for becoming a Successful Youth. In computer, he wrote the title "Understanding the Usefulness of Computer in the Twenty-first Century". In the area of Metallurgical and Materials engineering, he has the titles: The Performance of Loofah Fiber in Mortar: A Pilot study on the Compressive, Tensile and Flexural Strengths, Metallurgical and Materials Engineering: Introduction and Applications, and Powder Metallurgy: Its Engineering Consideration and Applications on Copper. He has written other books not mentioned here.

His voice is creative. His ideas are outstanding. His written articles are loved by readers from different parts of the world. His articles are not just combination of words but very informative as they are backed up with proper research works. He has been given writing projects by readers within and outside his country of origin and he delivered. You can confirm that his works are outstanding through his free articles on Hubpages United States and its affiliate sites on corruption, corruption in Nigeria, challenges in Nigeria, Kidnapping, just to mention but a few. His written works have been read by over 1.7 million people all over the world.

About the Book

This book is a part of the parent book "Nigerian Youth Challenges". This section is created to address a particular area of interest which is internet fraud among Nigerian youths. It is an important topic and that is explored in this book. The trend of internet scam for over six years now is getting out of hand. Yahoo boys also known as G Boys are going deeper into scam as days progress. These young scammers who are desperate of money have scammed many people and few of the victims committed suicide because of the large amount of money they lost.

Chapter one of the book is an introduction on who these fraudsters are and the popular names they answer while the chapter two is the confirmed incidences of the actions of the criminals in an outside the country. The information is sourced from reliable companies that report news and facts of incidences that happen in the world. Some of the incidences involved shedding of the blood of innocent

Nigerians because some of the so call Yahoo boys have advanced into killing of humans for rituals. It is believed that this kind of ritual makes them make more money through their wicked tricks.

Chapter three and four is on "terms and tricks used by Yahoo boys" and "how to avoid being a G guy" respectively. These young fraudsters in Nigeria speak in codes. They have terminologies they use when they do not want someone that is not part of their circle to understand. Also, they have tricks they apply for both their international and local scams. As a youth, there are things you have to know to avoid being a member of these internet scammers. These are explained in chapter four.

Chapter five and six focuses on "who are duped by Yahoo boys" and "funny things Yahoo boys do" respectively. Internet fraudsters cannot have everyone as their prey. For example, someone who is not exposed on the things happening in the world of internet can fall prey to the tricks of these get rich quick young men in Nigeria.

Also, there are some funny things that they do as well. These funny things may seem crazy to reasonable person but it is a big deal to some of the internet scammers.

Chapter seven is on the "characteristics of internet scammers in Nigeria" while eight is on "how Yahoo boys have influenced Nigerian Security". Yahoo boys in Nigeria have similar way of doing things. If you are a citizen of Nigeria, sometimes you do not need a seer to tell you if a particular person is a scammer or not. You know them by their actions. Also, the security who are instituted to fight crime in the country have been incapacitated by these boys. Some police officers cannot act to bring these young criminals to book because they might have in one way or the other collected bribes from them.

There are reasons why many Nigerian youths are taking advantage of people to make money and fill their pockets. There are some factors or the causes of their dirty actions. These are covered in chapter nine. And in chapter ten, the author explains why Nigerian government is not serious with the fight against Yahoo boys who are in various cities of the country.

Contact the Author

Email: pmicheal2013@gmail.com

Facebook: facebook.com/uzochukwu.mike